Designing a
Web Page
Using HTML Fundamentals

Dr. Graceanne Capra, Phd, ND

Outskirts Press, Inc.
Denver, Colorado

HTML Fundamentals

To be used with the files provided via download at
HTTP://HTML.GRACECAPRA.COM/
Copyright, Disclaimer of Warranties and Limitation of Liability

Printed in the United States of America

Learn HTML quickly!

With this amazing tutorial you will learn how to quickly and easily create your own Web Pages and be up and running in days!

About the Author

Graceanne Capra, N.D., Ph.D. has been in the computer field for over 16 years and has attained a double Masters one being in Computer Science. She has been a Manager for an IT dept and been a Software and Hardware computer trainer. The series of HTML books written are to help those truly interested in learning from a beginners stand point and become more advanced. HTML FUNDAMENTALS is the first in a series of recent pursuits, with work progressing quickly on the follow-up.

TABLE OF CONTENTS:

About this book: 7
How to use this book: 7
Chapter 1: 9
What is HTML 9
   HYPER TEXT MARKUP LANGUAGE 9
   WHERE IS HTML USED? 10
BUILDING A WEB PAGE 11
   HTML 11
   Web Page. That's right only TWO things! *11*
   A TEXT EDITOR AND A WEB BROWSER. 11
   SAVE: 14
   VIEW IT AS IT WOULD APPEAR ON THE WEB: 14
Now onto HTML TAGS ☺ 16
   HTML ~ Basics *16*
The Four Basic tags that are required to create a Web Page: 18
   HTML 18
   HEAD 18
   TITLE 18
   BODY 18
Summary of Chapter 1: 23
Recap practice Exercise #1: 23
Chapter 2: 25
Working with Paragraph Marks 25
   <P> PARAGRAPH </P> 26

 BREAK </BR> 26
   <PRE> PREFORMATTED </PRE> 26
Style Headings 28
   H1 (HEADING 1) 28
   H1 BEING THE LARGEST 28
   AND 28
   H6 (HEADING 6) 28
Formatting text 29
   <B> BOLD </B> 29
   <I> ITALIC </I> 29
   <U> UNDERLINE </U> 29
   <B> BOLD </B> 29
   <I> ITALIC </I> 29
Summary of Chapter 2: 30
Recap practice Exercise #2: 30

Chapter 3: **33**
WORKING WITH THE BODY ATTRIBUTES: 33
WORKING WITH COMMENTS: 33
WORKING WITH THE HORIZONTAL RULE: 33
LISTS: 35
SOME FREE ANIMATION SITES TO VISIT: 35
Summary of Chapter 3: **36**
Recap practice Exercise #3: **36**
Chapter 4: **38**
ADDING IMAGES 38
JPEG 38
GIF 38
BMP 38
Summary of Chapter 4: **40**
Recap practice Exercise #4: **40**
Chapter 5: **42**
Adding Links **42**
LINK TO A WEB PAGE 43
LINK TO A IMAGE 43
LINK TO A E-MAIL ADDRESS 43
Summary of Chapter 5: **44**
Recap practice Exercise #5: **44**
Chapter 6: **47**
SOUND **47**
ARE WE WIRED FOR SOUND YET! 47
TO ADD A BACKGROUND SOUND 47
Summary of Chapter 6: **49**
Recap practice Exercise #6: **49**
Some Websites to visit for HTML reference **52**
Download Sites **53**
Image Programs: **53**
Images/Animation: **53**
Summary of Tags **55**

About this book:

Think of this book as a friendly, approachable guide to learning the fundamentals of creating a Web Page using HTML. With the knowledge given in this book you will be able to build a readable, attractive Web Page or Web Site for the World Wide Web! Although HTML is not extremely hard to learn, it does pack a plethora of details. I look at HTML as I look at any Language ☺ Italian, French, Polish, Chinese….. Once you learn how to speak it, all will go together smoothly!

How to use this book:

This book tells you first what you will need to create a Web Page and then teaches you how to use HTML to get your page up and running on the World Wide Web. I will tell you what you will need to design and build effective Web documents that can bring your ideas and information to the whole on-line world…if that's what you want to do – You've got the information at your fingertips!

You will find downloadable practice files at
→**http://html.gracecapra.com/**
You will use these files to have hands-on practice throughout the book. I would suggest working and creating all your files into this downloaded folder and save the folder onto your computers DESKTOP ☺. Once you unzip the file you will see the folder is named "HTMLFundamentals_Recaps"

I suggest that you save all your practice files into this same folder, as all the files must be in the same folder and or same location in order for your Web Pages, files, pictures and everything to work! And should you question any of the exercises you work on, simply look in the downloaded folder and you can peek into the "CHEAT_SHEATS" folder for the exact code ;-) BIG SMILE!!! Also Throughout this book you will see items appear in a grey highlight, those are for you to do as a participant. For example SMILE ☺ so you should have smiled!!! OK now we know how the book and the files work Sooo, *let's get started!*

Chapter 1:

What is HTML

Hyper Text Markup Language

The Hyper Text Markup Language (HTML) is a series of standard codes and conventions designed to create pages and emphasize text for display in programs like Web Browsers. HTML is the basis of the World Wide Web, a global service of the Internet. The Web is the most graphical of all Internet services, allowing users to create their own Web Pages, using HTML.

Every HTML document is nothing more than a plain text document. There are no images or multimedia in an HTML document. Instead, the document points to the image files, which must be individually available alongside the HTML document.

So, when a viewer (like a Web Browser) reads the HTML document, it will also read instructions for loading and positioning any images or multimedia files that you've decided to include. To create an HTML document then, all you really need are the same tools you'd use to create a plain text document ---as you will soon see. ☺

A Web Page is a single HTML document, regardless of its length.

A Web Site is a number of HTML pages linked together and controlled by a particular individual or organization.

Although the scope and importance of HTML has changed somewhat over the past few years, its basic purpose is still the same. HTML is designed to create attractive, multimedia, electronic publications, specifically for the World Wide Web.

Where is HTML used?

Aside from the World Wide Web (which is overwhelmingly the major use of HTML), HTML is beginning to become popular in other parts of the Internet as well. For Instance:

- ❖ Some e-mail programs have begun to support certain commands in HTML.
- ❖ Some of the Internet's Usenet discussion groups also support HTML
- ❖ Some programs and operating systems are beginning to use HTML to format their online help documents.
- ❖ Some programs allow the use of HTML for discussion posts to other members, such as myspace.
- ❖ Companies often use HTML to create Intranets. Or Internet-like networks within their companies, for posting announcements, product information, and other important documents.

Generally, these are more limited uses of HTML – perhaps a few codes are used to change regular text into italic or to include a clickable hyperlink to an interesting Web Site. For Web authors, HTML tends to get rather involved, since there are a lot of interesting commands available for Web Pages and sites.

BUILDING A WEB PAGE

Aside from the knowledge of:

HTML

You need only two things in order to create a Web Page. That's right only TWO things!

A Text Editor and a Web Browser.

Neither of these programs should be very hard to find. Surprisingly, you don't need a connection to the WWW to create your Web Page. However, you will eventually want to have a connection in order to upload your pages onto the WWW. You will of course want your family, friends and other people around the world to be able to view your Web Pages.

❖ A **Text Editor** program let's you type text – that is, words, numbers, and symbols.
A powerful Text Editor with lots of features is called a Word Processor, for an example Microsoft Word. However, it is not recommended that you use a Word Processor to

type your HTML documents. These programs sometimes put codes into the text that a Web Browser can not understand, and they do not always save your file in such a way that a Web Browser can easily find it. A simple Text Editor is the best to use. Fortunately everyone who owns a computer with any version of Windows has the Text Editor **Notepad!** Notepad comes with the Windows software program.... You could also use Write, or WordPad. If you use a Macintosh, you should have a text editor called SimpleText.

Following is an example of a HTML document typed within Notepad.

<HTML>

<HEAD>

<TITLE>MY WEB PAGE</TITLE>

</HEAD>

<BODY>

Everything I want on my page goes here!

</BODY>

</HTML>

Throughout the following exercises we will be using Windows and Notepad...If you are running a Mac please *note* there may be slight differences.

Once you have found a good Text Editor, all you have to do is run it and start typing.
For instance, go to START on your windows task bar up to PROGRAMS and then up and over into ACCESSORIES then over and down to NOTEPAD.
In Notepad, TYPE the following exactly as it follows:

<html>
<head>
<title>My first Web Page</title>
</head>

<body>
This is an HTML heading.
The P in the angle brackets stands for Paragraph breaks. It is going to put your text onto the next line. Anything that I type in the body of this page that isn't between angle brackets will become part of my first Web Page!
</body>
</html>

You can now STOP TYPING.

SAVE:

Go to **FILE** on your pull down menu and select **SAVE AS** save this file onto your computers **desktop** into your downloaded practice files which the folder should be named HTML_Fundamentals_Recaps now name your brand new file **page1.html** (file names are case sensitive!)

(The html at the end of the name indicates that it contains HTML information.) The **html** extension let's the file be viewed in a Web Browser.

Some programs and people prefer to use an extension of **htm** which is also allowable.

CONGRATULATIONS! You've created your first Web Page!

View it as it Would Appear on the WEB:

❖ **A Web Browser**

Next, you'd probably like to see how this page would appear if it were on the World Wide Web (WWW). To do that, you will need a Web Browser. A Web Browser is the program you use to view pages on the WWW. Basically, it is a program that translates files written in HTML into neatly formatted text with pictures on your computer screen. If you have been on the WWW, then you have used a Web Browser. However, you may not be aware that you can also use a Web Browser to view HTML documents right from your hard drive. And that is why you can develop a Web Page without being connected to the Web (you do not need to be on-line).

Four popular Web Browsers are **Internet Explorer**, **Netscape Navigator**, **Opera**, and **Mozilla Firefox**

To download

Internet Explorer 6.0, 7.0 go to:
http://www.microsoft.com/windows/ie/downloads/default.mspx

Netscape 6.2, 8.1 go to:
http://browser.netscape.com/ns8/

Opera 6.01, 8.5 go to: http://www.opera.com

To Develop a Web Page, you will need to run your Text Editor and your Web Browser at the same time, as you will soon see!

We already saved our first Web Page.... so now let's take a look and get started on our HTML! Let's go **OPEN** our downloaded folder **(Html_Fundamentals_Recaps)** so that we may view our newly designed Web Page - **double click** onto our **"page1"** as you will see it opens up in Internet Explorer as a Web Page! We now want to add pictures, colors, sounds.... We need to work in our HTML.... From Internet Explorer go to **VIEW** on the Pull down menu and then down to **Source**. This opens up your Source Code (HTML) in Notepad! You will continue to work this way. You will modify your HTML in Notepad - always **SAVE** after you make a change, then go into Internet Explorer and click onto **REFRESH**, that will show all of your changes on your Web Page!

Now onto HTML TAGS ☺

HTML ~ Basics

The commands (known as **TAGS**) are enclosed in angle brackets < >. The tags normally come as a set. One to open a command, and one to close it. Everything between the two tags will be affected by them. The closing tag uses a forward slash / in it.

<TAG>   </TAG>

Tags are made up of **elements, properties,** and **values**. The command letters or words are called **elements**. Some elements have declared settings called **properties**. These properties help describe or shape the way the element will work or function. The property settings are known as **values**. Some tags can have many properties, others have none.

<ELEMENT PROPERTY="value">

Note : HTML tags are **not** case sensitive. You can use upper and/or lower case letters. In some studies, it shows tags are easier to recognize when they are in upper case (capitalized). But remember files such as, page names, pictures, and links are case sensitive!

The first step in building a Web Page is entering the **FOUNDATION** tags. These are the ground level commands that make up the **structure** of the Web Page code.

```
<HTML>
<HEAD>

<TITLE> </TITLE>

</HEAD>
<BODY>

</BODY>
</HTML>
```

The general rule with HTML tags is : For every beginning, there is an ending. The tags shown with the forward slash in them / are the ending tags.

The Four Basic tags that are required to create a Web Page:

HTML

This Web Page is written in Hyper Text Markup Language, and **All** Web Pages are written in this language. So this will be your very first Tag to start your page and when you are ready to end your page it will also be the very last tag that you will close.

HEAD

An introduction to your Web Page. In this area, some of the settings for your Web Page are introduced such as the TITLE, and information needed for search engines and subject directories.

TITLE

The title for your Web Page. Every good page deserves a name. This name will appear in the title bar at the top of the browser window. It is also used as the file name if someone 'bookmarks' your page or saves it as a favorite.

BODY

The Body is the main program section for your Web Page. This is where it all happens. Everything that people will see on your page goes here, within the body~!

❖ We start an HTML page with the simple phrase (code) inside our angle brackets: (known as tags) the first tag being **<html>**

❖ After that we state our page's title (this title goes on the Very top title bar on the top of your page). Notice that these tags surround the title but the one tag at the end has a slash before the code, that is because every tag must open and close. The "/" represents the end of your title: **<title>Your Page Title</title>**

❖ Again, notice the "/" before the second usage of "title". This "/" tells the browser that this is the end of the page's title. You will learn to use the "/" for almost all of the HTML tags. Because almost every tag must open and then close. The "/" closes the tag to say that you are done with that area.

❖ Next we type in the:
<body>

Now this body tag has different sub-sections. A sub-section is written into the tag like this:
<body subsection="something">
Also known as
<element property="value">

Most HTML tags have sub-sections or properties. However, sub-sections are usually not mandatory to use. The body tag has the following sub-sections:

❖ Remember that <Body will go before each of these subsections>

❖ Like <body Background="image.gif">

<body background="image.gif"> - The background image
<body bgcolor="#rgb_code"> - The background color
<body text="#rgb_code"> - The text color
<body link="#rgb_code"> - The text-link color
<body vlink="#rgb_code"> - The visited text-link color
<body alink="#rgb_code"> - The active text-link color

These can also all be written within one tag – an example how that would be coded:
<Body bgcolor="#ffffff" text="red vlink="blue">

❖ Now what is "rgb_code"? "Rgb_code" is a six digit code which signifies the color of something on the computer. The RGB stands for Red, Green and Blue. It is the way that your computer understands and reads colors. We will discuss the RGB in more detail in HTML Intermediate and the Advanced Books.

❖ And once you learn JavaScript you can write JavaScipt and the rgb_codes can be replaced by the name of the color. This is a lot easier ☺ but again you need to know JavaScript.

Here are a few examples of the Rgb color codes:

Red - ff0000
Green - 00ff00
Blue - 0000ff
Black - 000000
Yellow - ffff00

Within the downloaded materials provided at
http://html.gracecapra.com
You will have a Picture file with the RGB color
chart on it, the picture is titled: "rgbhex chart.gif".
Also…Some sites to visit to view the Rgb color chart:

http://www.snowcrest.net/dougbnt/colrtab.html

http://www.hypersolutions.org/pages/rgbhex.html

❖ After the BODY tag, the visible HTML is
shown as well as just plain text. Nothing special
is needed to display text other than typing it in
on your keyboard, however there are certain
HTML tags which you must put in for the text
to be shown in a certain way, also to put in
images, and other marks, you will learn these
tags in the next few exercises.

After you have placed all your visible HTML
and text, you must now close up the HTML
document. You do this by stating two things…

</body>
</html>

If you recall, I said that the slash "/" indicates
the close of the attribute. Thus, the tags above
tell the browser that this is the end of the visible
body and the end of the HTML document. They
are the only two tags that start at the beginning
and end at the very end of the HTML document.
Thus, combining all we have learned, this is
what a very basic HTML document's layout
looks like...

```html
<html>
<head>
<title>The Page's Title</title>
</head>
<body bgcolor="#ffccff"
text="#aaaaaa"
link="#00bb00">
This is where the visible HTML
tags and text goes.
</body>
</html>
```

Summary of Chapter 1:

Summary of Tags in this Chapter		
HTML TAG	**CLOSE TAG**	**MEANING**
<HTML>	</HTML>	Defines a Web-Formatted File
<HEAD>	</HEAD>	HTML Formatting Information
<TITLE>	</TITLE>	Title Bar
<BODY>	</BODY>	Body of the HTML page

Recap practice Exercise #1:

1. Create a Web Page using the four basic tags. *For an example*(refer to page 18-19)

2. On your Web Page use the TITLE I'm Great! Remember the title is for
your title bar on the top of your browser window. ☺

3. In the Body of your Web Page type This Is Great!

4. Save your Web Page as Page2.html on your computers desktop into your folder. *For an example*(refer to page 14)

Continue to next page please.

5. Open and view your Web Page using Internet Explorer or the browser of your choice. *For an example*(refer to page 15)

6. Change your Title to "This Is Great" save your changes, refresh your page and then review your page and the changes you have made.

7. Save and close all your windows.

Chapter 2:

Working with Paragraph Marks

OPEN your folder
("HTML_Fundamentals_Recaps") and then, please
OPEN the Web Page **html.html**

Let's first view the page and then view the source code. To view the source code, go to **VIEW** on your pull down menu and then to **SOURCE**. Remember to make any changes on your page you must be working in the source code, and always remember to SAVE your work then REFRESH your Web Page!

To have text show up onto your Web Pages you simply type what you want into your source code after the BODY <Body> tag. To get your text to go onto another line or to begin another paragraph you must use **Paragraph marks**: such as the Paragraph tag <P> and the Break Tag <BR>. These are two of the few tags that do not require a close tag....I do recommend always to close when you are first starting out, just to practice good habits! These are also the most commonly used tags, as you must tell the html code that you want a carriage return and/or a new paragraph.

To have your text enter down a whole paragraph (Two spaces) you will use the **Paragraph Tags:**

<p> Paragraph </p>

To have your text enter down to the very next line you will use the **Break Tags:**

 Break </br>

To get your text to appear exactly as you type it you must use **Preformatted Information Text Tags**:

<pre> Preformatted </pre>

Now that we have examined the html.html page let's work with a couple of examples:
Working in your **html.html source code**, under the closing **</h1> tag TYPE** the following text exactly as it appears, be sure to enter down to the next paragraph ☺.

TYPE
Today is a great day and I will also have a great night.

Tomorrow the weather is forecasted to be hot and sunny!

SAVE your work on your source code → **Close Notepad**, go onto Internet Explorer and **REFRESH** your changes to see how the text is displayed.

Did they show up on two separate lines as you typed it? The answer is "no" because you must use the paragraph tags <p>open and close </p>.
Go back to your source code, now and **TYPE** the <p> tag in-between the two sentences and a closing </p> tag.

Like so... Today is a great day and I will also have a great night.   <p> Tomorrow the weather is forecasted to be hot and sunny! </p>

SAVE → **Close** Notepad and then **REFRESH** your Web Page. You will now find that the sentences are on separate paragraph lines, as you wanted them to be. Go back into your source code and under the very bottom <br> tag **TYPE** the following word exactly as you see it.

S
 L
  A
   N
    T

You want the word to go down on the page and on a slant, **SAVE** your work on your source code → **Close** Notepad and then **REFRESH** your Web Page to view the results.

Ahhhaa... NO...it does not go down nor at a slant, you must use the <pre> </pre>tags!
With the <pre> tags you will find that the text will go anyway you place it!
Let's try the same thing using the <pre></pre>tags surrounding the Text.

So now go into your source code and **TYPE**

<pre>
S
  L
   A
    N
     T
</pre>

Ok we are ready to SAVE, go to **File → SAVE → Close** Notepad and in Internet Explorer **REFRESH** your page.

Style Headings

Your Style headings in HTML go from
H1 Through H6.

H1 (Heading 1)
H1 being the largest
and
H6 (Heading 6)
H6 being the smallest

Working in your html.html source code under the closing **</pre>** tag let's **TYPE**

<h1> This is a Heading </h1>
<h2> This is a Heading </h2>

continue to **TYPE** the same text for each heading <H3 – H6> putting each on a separate line.
SAVE the changes → **Close** Notepad and then go back to your Web Page **REFRESH** and view your changes.

Formatting text

<b> for Bold - <i> for Italic - <u> for Underline!

<b> Bold </b>
<i> Italic </i>
<u> Underline </u>

Now let's change some of our text so that they will appear bold, italic, and underlined.
Go into your html.html source code, and under the last closing heading tag</h6>
let's **TYPE**

<b> Bold </b>
<i> Italic </i>
<u> Underline </u>

SAVE the changes → **Close** Notepad and then go back to your Web Page **REFRESH** and view your changes.

Summary of Chapter 2:

Summary of Tags in this Chapter		
<P>	</P>	Paragraph break
 	</BR>	Line Break
<PRE>	</PRE>	Preformatted information
<H1> through <H6>	</H1> Through </H6>	Document style Headings
<B>	</B>	Bold
<I>	</I>	Italic
<U>	</U>	Underline

Recap practice Exercise #2:

1. Create a Web Page using the four basic tags. *For an example*(refer to page 18-19)

2. Use the Title Membership and Billing.

3. On your Web Page type the following paragraphs exactly as you see them:

Continue to next page please.

Nevertheless, if you want to highlight certain words, or phrases, titles, names, or other information, you'll learn how to do that within the hypertext Markup language before you finish this chapter.

To highlight your words, phrases, title, etc. you will use:
B
  O
    L
    D

BOLD
Italic
<u>Underline</u>

Do not type this:
Hint...The word Bold is Bold
The word Italic is Bold and Italic
The word Underline is Bold, Italic and Underlined

Continue to next page please.

Continue to TYPE this paragraph in your source code so that it will look exactly as you see it below:

Heading 1
Heading 2
Heading 3

4. Save your Web Page as Page3.html in your folder ("html fundamentals"). *For an example*(refer to page 14)

5. Open and view your Web Page using Internet Explorer.
   For an example(refer to page 15-16)

6. Change your Title to Great2 Save your changes, refresh your page and review your page and the changes you have made.

7. Save and close all your windows.

Chapter 3:

Working with the Body Attributes:
Working with Comments:
Working with the Horizontal Rule:

The first Body attribute is your body background color

<body bgcolor="#cccccc">

Your background color will be determined using the RGB Color Chart.

Not only can you use a color for your background you can also use Pictures.

<body background="picture.gif">

OPEN HTML2.html in your folder.

Go to your source code and **DELETE** your body **<body>** tag in its place **TYPE**
<body bgcolor="#cfffff"> **SAVE** your work **CLOSE** out of your source code, and once back into Internet Explorer **REFRESH** your Web Page and view your beautiful new background color!

Let's change the color to "#ccccff" **SAVE** and then **REFRESH** to see the new color!

Go back into your source code, do you see the code
<!--body bgcolor="#9a9a9a" this is grey-->
That background color code was already written in – but it did not show up on your Web Page....The reason for that is the **!** - - and the- - at the beginning and the end of the code. That makes anything inside your brackets a comment tag. Comments are only seen by you the "Web Master" ☺! Comments are a good way to makes notes for yourself!

Go to the bottom of your text and **TYPE**
<! -- Have a great day-- > **SAVE** → **Close** Notepad and **REFRESH** to view your page. You will never see comment tags on a Web Page, you will only see them in the source code. Also did you notice the Horizontal Rule tag <HR> it puts in a Horizontal line to break things up on your Web Page.

Go into your source code and **TYPE** <hr> after your first sentence. **SAVE** and **REFRESH** to see that you have added a horizontal rule!

LISTS:

Take a look on your page and you will see the

bulleted list.

In HTML lists are either Ordered Lists<OL> </OL>
or Unordered Lists <UL> </UL>
And then you must define each line as a List <Li></Li>.

Let's create a list go into your source code and
place your cursor after the comment tag
<!--Have a great day--> and **TYPE**

```
<OL>
<Li>HTML Fundamentals</Li>
<Li>HTML Intermediate</Li>
<Li>HTML Advanced</Li>
</OL>
```

SAVE and **CLOSE** your work and once back into
Internet Explorer **REFRESH** to view your lovely
ordered list, and the unordered list that was already
on your page!

Some free animation sites to visit:

http://www.animation-station.com/

http://www.animation-central.com/

http://www.syruss.com/

Summary of Chapter 3:

Summary of Tags in this Chapter		
HTML TAG	**TAG CLOSE**	**Description**
<body bgcolor="#cccccc">	</body>	Puts a color on the background of your page
<body background="picture.gif">	</body>	Puts a picture on the background of your page
<HR>	</HR>	Horizontal Rule
<!- - inside -->		Comment Tag
<OL>	</OL>	Ordered List
<Li>	</Li>	List
<UL>	</UL>	Unordered List

Recap practice Exercise #3:

1. Create a Web Page using the four basic tags. *For an example*(refer to page 18-19)

2. Use the title HelpDesk.

3. On your Web Page type the following paragraphs exactly as you see them:

Continue to next page please.

TYPE this paragraph:
To highlight your words, phrases, title, etc. you will use:

B
  O
    L
     D

BOLD
Italic
<u>Underline</u>

4. Make your background color a pink shade.

5. Put in a comment that reminds you of the RGB code for a blue color.

6. Put a Horizontal Rule on your page. *For an example*(refer to page 34)

7. Save your page as Page4.html in your folder then view your Web Page to make sure that you have everything correct! *For an example*(refer to page 14)

Chapter 4:

Adding Images

Putting images on your pages will spice it up! Keep in mind that the larger the image file the longer it will take to load your page. Also keep in mind, every file on the computer has a three letter extension associated with it. Common Picture files are:

JPEG
GIF
BMP

The BMP image files typically are larger files, so you will not want to use too many BMP files.

When adding images to your page keep in mind that although html is not case sensitive file names are!

OPEN up Internet Explorer and **GO TO** WWW.ALTAVISTA.COM
Once on Altavista click onto the IMAGE tab and then click into the search box and **TYPE** "smiley" for your search selection then click search. Find an image you like and **SAVE** it in your folder. To SAVE your image from the Internet you will right click onto the image and select SAVE picture as. Then you will change the name to something short and simple that you will remember.

Keep in mind, file names are case sensitive and you must know the 3 letter extension. Eg. "Sun.jpg" would be a name of an image, also be sure to SAVE your image in your downloaded folder.

Let's **OPEN** HTML2.html and go to the source code in our source code we are going to add the image we just saved.

To add the image, we will **TYPE** **<img src="nameofimage.jpg">**at the end of the text in the body of our page. **SAVE →REFRESH** and view your Web Page and your beautiful image.

Now let's center our image by doing the following: **TYPE**

** <img src="nameofimage.jpg"> **

SAVE →REFRESH and view your page.

Summary of Chapter 4:

Summary of Tags in this Chapter		
HTML TAG	TAG CLOSE	Description
\<img src="name.jpg">		Puts image on your page
\<center>	\</center>	Centers
\<img src="name.jpg" align=left>		Aligns image to the left
\<img src="name.jpg" align=right>		Aligns image to the right

Recap practice Exercise #4:

1. Create a Web Page using the four basic tags.
   For an example(refer to page 18-19)

2. Use the title AWESOME.

3. On your Web Page type the following paragraphs exactly as you see them:

Continue to next page please.

It is great to see you creating your own **WEB PAGE**. Soon you will have your own site for everyone to view out on the Internet!

G
  R
   E
   A
    T

Design!

4. Make your background any Shade you would like.

5. Put in a comment that reminds you of the RGB code for a Red color.

6. Put a Horizontal Rule on your page. *For an example*(refer to page 34)

7. Put your image that you saved from the Internet on your page and center the image. *For an example*(refer to page 38-39)

8. Save your page as Page5.html in your folder then view your Web Page to make sure that you have everything correct! *For an example*(refer to page 14)

Chapter 5:

Adding Links

On every Web Page on the Internet/Intranet you will find *Hyperlinks*, also known as links to other pages. On Web Pages you will click your mouse onto those links to go to other Web Pages. Hyperlinks can be text or Images. A Hyperlink to another Web Page is the equivalent to you turning pages within a paperback book. Hyperlinks are usually Blue in color and underlined. Another indication is when you scroll your mouse over a hyperlink it will change from a pointer to a hand.

OPEN up HTML3.html view the contents on the Web Page and then go into the source code.
We are looking for the link tags
<a href="nameoflink.html"> the text people click onto</a>
You must make sure you close your link tags or they will not work!

Let's take a closer look at this link tag
<a href> stands for anchor, href stands for hyper reference, and then we add the value type the text or image we want viewers to see and then we must close the anchor </a>

Link to a Web Page

We are going to create a link to html.html, so let's go into our source code and at the bottom of our body **TYPE** **<a href="html.html">Back to our INDEX</a>**

SAVE, →REFRESH your Web Page and then test your link.

Link to a Image

Go back into your source code and let's look at the image link....

Let's create an image link, **TYPE**

<a href="Golf.html"><img src="golf.gif"></a>
SAVE it and test it!

Link to a E-mail address

Now we want to add an e-mail link....

you will **TYPE** the following on the bottom of your Web Page

<center>
<a href="mailto:askme@gracecapra.com">
<img src="email.gif"></a>
</center>

take notice that we are centering the e-mail image. It could be text or an image just like every link!

SAVE your work, **REFRESH** your page and view your changes! Notice that when you set your mouse onto any link including the e-mail in the lower left corner of your window (status bar) you will see where your link is going!

Summary of Chapter 5:

Summary of Tags in this Chapter		
HTML TAG	**TAG CLOSE**	**Description**
<a href="page.html">	</a>	Puts a link onto your page to another page
<a href="page.html"> <img src="image.gif">	</a>	Links an to another page
<a href="mailto:yourmail @aol.com">	</a>	E-mail link

Recap practice Exercise #5:

1. Create a Web Page using the four basic tags.
   For an example(refer to page 18-19)

2. Use the title Customer Service

3. On your Web Page type the following paragraphs exactly as you see them:

Continue to next page please.

Now you are adding images and linking pages!!!

T
 H
  I
   S
I
S

G
 R
  E
   A
    T

Design!

4. Make your background any Shade you would like.
   For an example(refer to page 20)

5. Put in a comment that reminds you of the RGB code for a light grey color. *For an example*(refer to page 34)

Continue to next page please.

6. Put a Horizontal Rule on your page. *For an example*(refer to page 34)

7. Put your image that you saved from the Internet on your page and Left align the image. *For an example*(refer to page 38-39)

8. Add the image fish.gif to your page, and make that image link to your Page5.html page. *For an example*(refer to page 43)

9. Let's now add an e-mail link to your page going to "yourname@aol.com"
   Use the image "email.gif" to link your e-mail address to.
   For an example(refer to page 43)

10.Save your page as Page6.html in your folder then view and try your links on your Web Page to make sure that you have everything correct and working!
   For an example(refer to page 14)

Chapter 6:

SOUND
ARE WE WIRED FOR SOUND YET!

To add a background sound
You are going to find that just like most computer tasks... there are three ways to do many things! Adding sound onto your pages can be done in several ways... you can simply have background sound. You can have background sound with an image. You can have video with sound.....Right now we are going to see how to set background sound and how to embed a video with sound!

you will add the following tag :
<embed src="name of sound.wav" autostart=true loop=true hidden=false>

Let's **OPEN** up **HTML3.html** and add the following tag under the <body> tag,
TYPE <embed src="Eric.AVI" autostart=true loop=true hidden=false>

the tag is telling the browser to embed the sound.
autostart=true
that is saying start playing automatically
loop= true
is telling the browser to continue to play the sound over and over again! Hidden=false
is telling the browser we do not want to see any of the controls

So now let's go back into our source code and make some changes.

Let's change the tag to read **TYPE** **<embed src="Eric.AVI" autostart=true loop=true hidden= False>**

SAVE, →**REFRESH** your work and let's view and listen to our changes!

Summary of Chapter 6:

Summary of Tags in this Chapter		
HTML TAG	**TAG CLOSE**	**Description**
<embed src="sound.wav">		Puts sound on your page!
<embed src="sound.wav" autostart=true>		Starts sound automatically
<embed src="sound.wav" loop=true>		Keeps playing the sound over and over
<embed src="sound.wav" hidden=true>		Hides the controls to the sound
<embed src="sound.wav" hidden=false>		Shows the controls to the sound

Recap practice Exercise #6:

1. Create a Web Page using the four basic tags.
   For an example(refer to page 18-19)

2. On your Web Page type the following paragraphs exactly as you see them:

Continue to next page please.

TYPE the following:

Now you are adding images, linking pages and you are WIRED FOR SOUND!!!

T
 H
  I
   S
I
S

G
 R
  E
  A
   T

MUSIC!

3. Make your background any Shade you would like.

4. Put in a comment that reminds you of the RGB code for a light Green color. *For an example*(refer to page 34)

Continue to next page please.

5. Put a Horizontal Rule on your page.
   For an example(refer to page 34)

6. Put your image that you saved from the Internet on your page and right align the image.
   For an example(refer to page 39-40)

7. Add the image sun.gif to your page, and make that image link to your Page6.html page.
   For an example(refer to page 43)

8. Add a link to Page5.html.
   For an example(refer to page 43)

9. Add a link to Page4.html.
   For an example(refer to page 43)

10. Add background sound to your page.
    For an example(refer to page 47)

11. **Save your page as Page7.html in your folder then view and listen to YOUR Fancy new Web Page!**

Now that we have all our Basics down we can go ahead and start customizing all of our options.... These more advanced tags will be covered in my continued series of books, Designing a Web Page using HTML Intermediate and Designing a Web Page using HTML Advanced!
See you then!!! ☺

Some Websites to visit for HTML reference

http://www.w3.org/ -- World Wide Web Consortium

http://www.htmlgoodies.com

http://archive.ncsa.uiuc.edu/General/Internet/WWW/HTMLPrimer.html

http://hotwired.lycos.com/webmonkey/reference/html_cheatsheet/

http://sunsite.berkeley.edu/Web/

Download Sites

http://html.gracecapra.com

http://downloads-zdnet.com.com/

http://www.download.com

http://www.microsoft.com/windows/ie/down loads/default.mspx

 http://browser.netscape.com/ns8/

http://www.opera.com

Image Programs:

http://www.xequte.com

http://www.smartdraw.com/specials/clipart.a sp?id=2258

Images/Animation:

http://www.freeimages.co.uk/

http://www.hellasmultimedia.com/webimag es/images-htm/image.htm

http://clipartuniverse.com/free-animation.shtml

Images/Animation: *con't*

http://www.animationonline.com/

http://www.animation.com/gt/homepage.asp

http://www.animationlibrary.com/a-l/

http://www.animationcity.net/animcity.htm

http://www.animation-station.com/

http://www.animation-central.com/

http://www.syruss.com/

Summary of Tags

Summary of Tags in Chapter 1		
HTML TAG	**Tag Close**	**MEANING**
<HTML>	</HTML>	Defines a Web-Formatted File
<HEAD>	</HEAD>	HTML Formatting Information
<TITLE>	</TITLE>	Title Bar
<BODY>	</BODY>	Body of the HTML page
Summary of Tags in Chapter 2		
<p>	</p>	Paragraph break
 	</br>	Line Break
<pre>	</pre>	Preformatted information
<H1> through <H6>	</H1> Through </H6>	Document style Headings
<b>	</b>	Bold
<I>	</I>	Italic
<U>	</U>	Underline
Summary of Tags in Chapter 3		
<body bgcolor="#cccccc">	</body>	Puts a color on the background of your page
<hr>	</Hr>	Horizontal Rule
<!- - inside -->		Comment Tag
<OL>	</OL>	Ordered List
<Li>	</Li>	List
<UL>	</UL>	Unordered List

Summary of Tags in Chapter 4		
HTML TAG	**TAG CLOSE**	Description
<img src="name.jpg">		Puts image on your page
<center>	</center>	Centers
<img src="name.jpg"		Aligns image to the

55

align=left>		left
<img src="name.jpg" align=right>		Aligns image to the right

Summary of Tags in Chapter 5		
HTML TAG	**TAG CLOSE**	**Description**
<a href="page.html">	</a>	Puts a link onto your page to another page
<a href="page.html"> <img src="image.gif">	</a>	Links an image to another page
<a href="mailto:gcapra@n yc.rr.com">	</a>	E-mail link

Summary of Tags Chapter 6		
HTML TAG	**TAG CLOSE**	**Description**
<embed src="sound.wav">		Puts sound on your page!
<embed src="sound.wav" autostart=true>		Starts sound automatically
<embed src="sound.wav" loop=true>		Keeps playing the sound over and over
<embed src="sound.wav" hidden=true>		Hides the controls to the sound
<embed src="sound.wav" hidden=false>		Shows the controls to the sound

www.ingramcontent.com/pod-product-compliance
Lightning Source LLC
Chambersburg PA
CBHW051115050326
40690CB00006B/792